HENRY WINKLER

A Little Golden Book® Biography

By Betsy Groban • Illustrated by Kayla Harren

For Ira: This one's for you. —G-Ma

 A GOLDEN BOOK • NEW YORK

Golden Books
An imprint of Random House Children's Books
A division of Penguin Random House LLC
1745 Broadway, New York, NY 10019
penguinrandomhouse.com
rhcbooks.com
Text copyright © 2025 by Betsy Groban
Cover art and interior illustrations copyright © 2025 by Kayla Harren
Golden Books, A Golden Book, A Little Golden Book, the G colophon, and the
distinctive gold spine are registered trademarks of Penguin Random House LLC.
Library of Congress Control Number: 2024949654
ISBN 978-0-593-81039-2 (trade) — ISBN 978-0-593-81040-8 (ebook)
Manufactured in the United States of America
10 9 8 7 6 5 4 3 2 1
EU Contact: Penguin Random House Ireland, 32 Nassau Street, Dublin D02 YH68.
https://eu-contact.penguin.ie.

Henry Franklin Winkler was born on October 30, 1945. He says that he grew up in "the great indoors" of New York City. His parents were German Jews who fled Europe during World War II. They owned a large lumber company and expected their son to join the family business. But for Henry, who always wanted to be an actor, the only wood that interested him was Hollywood.

As a boy, Henry struggled with schoolwork. He was smart, but he had trouble reading, spelling, writing, and pronouncing words. Henry's learning challenges made him feel bad about himself. Thankfully, he found something at school that made him happy: acting.

In kindergarten, Henry played a tube of toothpaste in a classroom show. In eighth grade, he was the star of *Billy Budd*, a play about a sailor. Reading lines was difficult for Henry, so he memorized as much as he could, and if he forgot the words, he improvised or made things up!

Henry got his high school diploma in 1963 with the help of a few great teachers who believed in him. He went on to get degrees from Emerson College and the Yale School of Drama.

After graduating from Yale, Henry auditioned for acting jobs. In one year, he was in more than thirty television commercials for everything from razors and coffee to insurance companies. The work earned him enough money to pay his bills so he could act in plays at night for free.

Henry's first big acting break was in a movie called *The Lords of Flatbush,* a drama about teenagers growing up in Brooklyn. Soon after filming the movie, Henry moved from New York to California and was cast in a TV series that would make him famous around the world!

Happy Days premiered on January 15, 1974. The comedy series was about a wholesome teenage boy named Richie Cunningham, growing up in Milwaukee in the 1950s. Henry played a mechanic named Arthur Fonzarelli, who everyone called Fonzie or the Fonz. Fonzie lived in an apartment above the Cunninghams' garage.

Before long, *Happy Days* was the number one show on television, and the Fonz was the most popular character. Everything he did was cool. He rode a motorcycle. He made a jukebox play music with one tap of his fist. He wore a leather jacket—even while waterskiing!

Fans imitated the Fonz by giving a thumbs-up and saying, "Aayyyy!"

When the *Happy Days* cast wasn't working, they traveled around playing softball. Henry had never played a team sport as a child. The other actors taught him how to pitch. He wasn't the best player, but he sure had fun!

Happy Days ran for ten years and changed Henry's life. During that time, he won two Golden Globe awards for playing the Fonz, and he received a star on the Hollywood Walk of Fame.

THE WATERBOY

CLICK

Henry took a break from acting after *Happy Days.* He wanted to play different characters, but he was only offered roles similar to the Fonz. So, he worked behind the camera instead, as a producer and director on shows including *MacGyver* and *Sabrina the Teenage Witch.*

In 1991, he started getting small roles in movies and TV shows again. He got to play a football coach, a dad, and a doctor. In 2003, Henry found great success playing a funny lawyer in the TV series *Arrested Development.*

Henry has been married to his wife, Stacey, since 1978. Together, they've raised three kids and have helped to improve the lives of thousands more by donating their time and money to charities. Along with a few other Hollywood celebrities, they started the Children's Action Network. The organization gave free vaccinations to 200,000 kids and currently helps find homes for children in foster care.

Maybe school is difficult, but when you get out, you **soar** like an eagle!

All of Henry and Stacey's kids have dyslexia—
a learning disability that makes it hard to read, spell,
and write. When his stepson was diagnosed, so was
Henry! He was relieved to finally discover the reason
for his lifelong reading difficulties. Henry wants all
children with dyslexia to know that they are smart
and can achieve great things.

Of his many accomplishments, Henry is most proud of the children's books he cowrote with Lin Oliver about a boy named Hank Zipzer. Hank is smart and funny and has learning differences. The books are inspired by Henry's childhood.

Some books in the *Here's Hank* series are printed with a font designed to be easier for people with dyslexia to read. The book you're reading right now uses a similar font!

The books starring Hank Zipzer are also popular in England. In 2011, Henry was made an Honorary Officer of the Most Excellent Order of the British Empire by Queen Elizabeth II for his work helping British children with dyslexia and other learning challenges.

In 2018, forty-four years after he became famous as the Fonz, Henry won his first Primetime Emmy Award! It was for his role as an acting teacher on the television series *Barry*. Henry was very proud.

When Henry isn't acting or writing, he loves spending time with his six grandchildren and fishing. He goes fly-fishing every year. Once, he caught sixty trout in a single day! Henry takes a picture of each fish before releasing it back into the water.

Henry Winkler is an award-winning actor, a bestselling author, and a loving husband, father, and grandfather. He is polite and kind and does what he can to make sure people always have *happy days.* No wonder he is often called the Nicest Man in Hollywood!